W9-ACV-934

3

provide accurate, up to date and reliable complete information. No warranties of any kind are expressed or implied. Readers acknowledge that the author is not engaging in the rendering of legal, financial, medical or professional advice. The content of this book has been derived from various sources. Please consult a licensed professional before attempting any techniques outlined in this book.

By reading this document, the reader agrees that under no circumstances are is the author responsible for any losses, direct or indirect, which are incurred as a result of the use of information contained within this document, including, but not limited to, —errors, omissions, or inaccuracies.

Job Interview: Land Your Dream Job by Conquering your Next Job Interview by Answering 50 Tough Job Interview Questions and Maximizing Your Resume and Cover Letter

Secrets To Unlock All The Right Answers During The Job Interview Process. Includes 50 Tough Job Interview Questions And How To Answer Them

Series: Job Pinnacle 2020

By: Freddy Palmer

JOB PINNACLE 2020

JOB INTERVIEW

Land Your Dream Job by Conquering Your Next Job Interview by Answering 50 Tough Job Interview Questions and Maximizing Your Resume and Cover Letter

FREDDY PALMER

Table of Contents

Introduction

Landing a good, well-paying job is perhaps, the foremost thought that occupies the minds of new job seekers, especially those who have just obtained a professional degree in a major of their choice. Their hearts and minds are filled with hope and excitement as they step out into the world looking for a place to start their career, based on the credentials they worked so hard to achieve.

One of the biggest hurdles that you will have to cross to land yourself a good job is the job interview. It consists of a meeting with people within the organization. This job interview allows both you and your employers to understand each other's expectations so that the professional relationship can start off on the right footing.

Job interviews are two-way streets allowing for a flow of information between the employer and the potential employee. It is the ultimate round that decides whether you will be hired by the employer and/or whether, in fact, you want to be hired by the employer.

In today's world, there have many changes that have taken place in regards to knowing how to conduct and master the job interview than there has been in the past twenty years. The aim of this book is to help you navigate and ensure that you are informed with the BEST way to conquer and maximize job offers by successfully completing the job interview. The methods that will be discussed will be valid for new and old generations in TODAY'S job market.

Features of a job interview

• Your chance of getting called for a job interview is based on your resume and/or cover letter that you send to the company as part of the job application process

• The company would scrutinize the resume and cover letter and then choose suitable candidates to call for the job interview

• So, your resume and the job interview together form the basis of your selection or rejection as a suitable candidate for the job

The job interview is, perhaps, the most critical measure that a company uses to decide and zero in on prospective employees. It is important to note that this is the final step in their process to hire you to be part of their workplace ecosystem. Furthermore, if you take one step back and from their perspective, you realize that if they hire you, they will provide you with income for the next foreseeable future. It is essentially a life-changing moment! So as exciting as it is to get a new job, the important memento to keep in mind is HOW MUCH you want this job and how the employer will provide a significant role into your life.

The Process Of A Job Interview

A job interview would usually comprise of the job seeker and a panel of two or more members of the company. The potential immediate boss is normally part of this panel. Usually, a human resources specialist or the one contacted you by phone or email is also included in the panel. Depending on the company and the role that you have applied for, there could be a single or multiple rounds of interviews conducted before the final decision to recruit is taken.

If the process consists of more than one round of interviews, then each level would have to be cleared by you before you can be called to the next level. The duration of an interview is highly dynamic and could range from 15 minutes to several hours. In fact, there are cases where interview rounds have lasted an entire day.

The questions that are asked are also highly varied and can range from the mundane "describe yourself" to something as profound as "If you were all alone in this world, what would be the first thing you would want to do?" Of course, technical questions based on the actual job are also invariably included in the interview process. This guide will focus on job interview questions and situations that is general in terms and not cover technical questions because everyone comes from a different background or industry. It is highly recommended to practice and review technical jargon based on your industry.

Irrespective of your domain of expertise, a job interview is the final and most critical aspect that decides whether you will land the job or not. While good grades may be important for the initial screening process, once you are called in for an interview, the grades are relegated to the background and how you handle yourself at the interview becomes the deciding factor.

This book is aimed at giving you different aspects to consider while preparing for a job interview. It gives you tips on how to avoid common mistakes, how to answer difficult questions with élan, how to sell yourself, and much more. By the time you finish reading and understand the content of this book, you will be more confident about yourself and what you need to do to make up for any gaps in your preparation process.

Chapter 1: Resume Vs. Cover Letter. Honing Each Components

While resumes and cover letters, by themselves, are not sufficient to get you a job, they are integral parts of the job seeking process. Resumes and cover letters are the first impressions that you create. An organization filters resumes and cover letters to call candidates for job interviews.

So, if your resume and cover letter are not impressive, then the chances that you get called for a job interview are quite low. It is, therefore, essential for you to spend some time and energy in making your resume look good enough for an organization to want to meet you in person.

Resume Versus Cover Letter

There is a vast different between the two and one cannot replace the other. A well-written set will work in tandem with each other resulting in impressing any potential employer. Although both the resume and the cover letter share the purpose of presenting you as a person highly suitable for the job applied for, there are key differences between the two elements.

A **resume** documents the history of your employment and has a summary of your educational qualifications, your previous job details, skill sets that you possess, certifications and other quantifiable aspects that are relevant to the job. A **cover letter**, on the other hand, contains additional information about you that presents you as a perfect candidate for the job.

The **format of a resume** usually includes the following sections:

• Personal information section – This contains your full name, postal address, and other contact information such as your email address and your phone number

• Educational qualification section – This has detailed descriptions of your educational qualifications, usually going backward and thus starting from the most recent. This section will include details of the year you got your degree, the name of the college you attended, etc.

- Experience section – This will have detailed descriptions of all your previous jobs. The details that are normally included are job titles of jobs that you held, years of experience in that particular job, positions, and functions of the job, etc.

- Other relevant skills section – This section will contain details of other skills and certifications that you have earned which are not covered elsewhere.

The *format of a cover letter* is like that of a formal letter and contains added information that makes you a perfect candidate for the job. The cover letter will have a salutation, multiple paragraphs and a closing paragraph. A cover letter should ideally be about 3-4 paragraphs long and should be written in such a way that your potential employer can easily consult your resume and find detailed information that matches what is there in the cover letter. Cover letters must be one page in length and no more. You do not want more than one page, as that will defeat its purpose. It should be brief and concise! One of the errors that new job seekers tend to do is disclosing too much personal info in their cover letters. It is not a story! Keep it brief and informative. Capture the employer's attention but also be informative. More content of what should be in the cover letter will be covered later.

Resumes on the hand, will be more objective in its outlook. A **cover letter** should include more subjective elements such as why you are interested in the job you are applying for, what and how your values motivate you, or how the company's culture appeals to you.

How To Write A Resume

Before you start to write your resume, ask yourself some basic questions such as:

- Are you an entry-level job seeker?

- Are you changing careers?

- Are you getting back to a career after a break?

Depending on the answers to the above questions, your resume process will change suitably. There are different types of resumes that you can use and some of them are listed below:

- ***Chronological resume*** – This is the most common type of resume that you will find and is written with details of your previous jobs in chronological order starting from the most recent and going backward in time. Employers are quite fond of this type as it gives them a convenient profile of your job history. This format is good for people with a long and strong job history.

- ***Functional resume*** – This type focuses on your skills rather than on your previous jobs and is good for people who are starting off on a new career, those who are looking for a career change or those who are getting back to work after a long sabbatical.

- ***Combination resume*** – This type first lists your skills and functions and then talks about your job history in chronological order.

- ***Targeted resume*** – This type of resume is specifically written to target one particular job and highlights your skills, expertise and experience that make you an ideal candidate for the targeted job.

The question now is, which type of resume should you make? There is actually a best answer to this and that is a targeted resume. The targeted resume is the best because it specializes the resumes to that particular job posting. By looking at the job posting, and taking keywords from it in making your resume, you are now exponentially increasing your chances of being selected than other generic types of resumes. The other types of resumes are "okay" too but they are may come off as 'standard' resumes that everyone else is using.

List Of Keywords That You Should Include In Your Resume

The keywords you use in your resume help in getting you selected for the job interview because hiring managers use these specific keywords to search for potential candidates. It is, therefore, imperative to include action verbs such as the following examples:

- <u>Proficient</u> in Microsoft Excel and Word

- <u>Specialized</u> in banking customer services

- <u>Helped</u> manage sales at the front desk area

Here are a few action verbs that you must try and include in your resume that will make your resume stand out:

Accomplished, achieved, allocated, aided, brainstormed, compiled, developed, facilitated, handled, illustrated, instilled, justified, launched, litigated, mediated, mastered, networked, negotiated, oversaw, obtained, pioneered, permitted, prioritized, procured, placed, proposed, questioned, qualified, resolved, revitalized, reversed, researched, scheduled, stabilized, steered, supervised, transformed, undertook, united, upgraded, validated, visualized, verified, worked, witnessed, won, welcome

The Key To Resumes Are Your Achievements

Believe it or not, the key to your resume is your achievements. Yes, it's important to note what you job you've done in the past, your education, as well as your skills and awards. However your achievements are the ones that potential employers look at the most. Furthermore, providing **evidence** whether they may be *quantitated* or *qualitative* are highly smiled upon by potential employers. Take a look at the following example below. Which one makes a more compelling for a job description in the resume?

Fedex Operations Manger (2017)

-Managed performance of 20 Fedex ground employees

-Complete audits of safety protocols

-Ensure dock metrics are met during monthly meetings.

OR

-Sustaining 90% approval job rating of 20 FedEx ground employees in Q4 in 2016.

-Meeting 100% of all occupational audits by both FedEx and government agencies

-Supervised 4 freight docks and ensuring high quality dock metric standards set by company standards

As you can see, by backing up your job description in your resume with tangible and hard data, it makes it much more vivid for employers to see what you've actually done. Furthermore, one of the things that most employers are guilty of is, the more "numbers" are shown in your resume, the better!

How to create a cover letter

It is absolutely essential to address your cover letter to a particular person. A general "Dear sir/madam" reflects your unprofessionalism. So, do some research and address your cover letter to the right person. Make sure your first paragraph is catchy and includes some details of the job you are applying for and your key skills that perfectly match the job's specifications.

In the subsequent paragraphs, you can go a little deeper and present data that adds value to your profile and demonstrates your suitability for the job at hand. You can also add some information that you know about the company that appeals to you. You should include how you plan to contribute to the company's growth and what value you can give to the organization in the role you intend to occupy.

Final Tips

It is imperative that you do a spell-check and a grammar-check on your resume and cover letter. Any kind of mistakes in basic communication mechanics is unforgivable. Moreover, your resume and cover letter will not even be looked at if these kinds of errors exist in them. So, spend some extra time on making sure your basic job application elements are free from spelling and grammatical errors.

Chapter 2: Researching The Job

Researching the job and finding out details of the potential employer are two critical aspects to consider very seriously if you want to stand out during the job interview. Investigating and collecting data and information about the company will empower you with plenty of ammunition that you can leverage during the job interview process.

Reasons For Researching The Job And The Company Before The Interview Process

There are many reasons why researching the job is important before your job interview happens. Some of the reasons include:

• It is a tool to build knowledge about the company and make your interview process a more rewarding one

• It helps you get some detailed insights into the working of the company which will come in useful to you when you are answering some difficult questions posed during the job interview

• Researching will help you know if the job post and/or the company are legitimate in all respects.

• It helps you understand other aspects of the company that may not be directly related to the job you are applying for but yet could be useful to get an edge over the competition

What are the things you must look for during your research process?

The following things about the job and company will help your job interview preparation process immensely giving you a good edge over other job seekers.

What are the skills and experience the company is looking for? – This is, perhaps, the first thing you must learn about the job. What are the skills and relevant experience the company is looking for in an ideal candidate? Using this information, you can position yourself as an ideal candidate for the job.

While this kind of information may or may not be overtly available for you to see and discover, if you delve a little deeply into the job posting or read between the lines, you are bound to get the information that you seek. Also, you can talk to and ask other employees working for the company.

Find out information about prominent players in the company – These people could include Senior Managers, directors of the various departments, the CEO and/or the President, etc. This information can be easily found in the "About" page of the company's website. You can also see what they are talking about and how they are trending on social media platforms.

In fact, you will be able to get a lot of feedback about these key company players from employees on social media platforms.

Furthermore, use the power of LinkedIn. You've heard stories of how employers look at your social media page to make sure everything "checks out." Well that actually works both ways. Take a look at the person who is interviewing you or those that might potentially speak with your during the job interview process. You can check their LinkedIn page to get background info of their professional career. Also, by knowing their degree and the university they went to, or even their previous positions, you can really strike a friendly conversation to break the ice, which actually makes you more likable. Of course, we're not stalking them, but just getting a jest of who they are.

Another secret that most people don't know about is LinkedIn is that you should match and update your *general* resume with your LinkedIn resume. This is because potential employers want an updated version of your digital self. If they see that you didn't have your most recent position in LinkedIn, it could be a 'red flag' for them as they start if you had an amicable relationship with your previous employer.

Find out about the latest news and updates about the company – It is nice to be armed with the latest information and recent events of the company before you venture out for the job interview. Most of the large corporate houses have a page on their website dedicated to the events and press releases. You can look up this page to get such information about the company.

Find out about the company's values, culture and mission - Most of the companies are seeking candidates whose values and culture are aligned to that of the company. This way, they can ensure that there is no conflict of interest between the employees and the organization thereby enhancing the chances for improved value.

It is, therefore, imperative that you learn about the organization's values, culture, and mission and position your own to that thereby giving yourself a much higher chance of landing the job. By reiterating this information in the job interview, you will not only impress them, but they will cognitively realize that you've done your due diligence of researching who they are!

Know about the company's products, services and clients – After all, the work you will be doing in the company will directly or indirectly affect the three components mentioned in this point: products, services and clients. Hence, knowing about these three elements with regard to your potential employer will help you customize your answers appropriately.

Additionally, if your skills and relevant experience include something that can have a positive impact on the company's relationship with one or more of its clients, then you can highlight these aspects during the interview process.

You can get information about the company's products and services from the website. You can find blogs and case studies and read and understand the company's way of doing things. Glassdoor.com is one of the better websites regarding these products, services, and clients. There are also very good previous employee reviews that quantify the likability of that employer.

Any relevant inside information – There are multiple sources to get such information. Knowing a present employee well can be a huge asset. However, there are also various websites such as Ziprecruiter, Indeed, and Glassdoor and also social media platforms where present and past employees may have left precious information that you could leverage to your advantage. If you dig a little deeper, you can find out salary details, traits and characteristics the company keeps a lookout for in a potential candidate, the interview process, duties and functions of the particular job, etc.

Find out about the person or people who are going to be on your interview panel – Such information will help you connect with them during the interview process and set up a good rapport with the panelists. While, initially, it may seem a rather daunting task to find out information about the interview panelists, a few investigative searches from you can yield good results.

One way is to use the email that has been sent to you regarding details of the job interview. If no information is available, then you can send an email politely asking who will be interviewing you. Once you get the name(s) of the interview panelists, you can look them up on LinkedIn and Twitter and know a little more about what they are passionate about and what drives them.

Let me assure you that this kind of knowledge that gives you an insight into the personality of the interviewer(s) is really powerful, which you can use to your advantage. This gives you a leading edge over other competitors.

Final Thoughts

While it is imperative that you research a job and the company before you go for the job interview, it is equally important to stay within limits and not go overboard during the interview process by overloading the panelists with all the data that you have managed to collect. It may make you look too curious.

You should use the data only when the time is opportune and/or it helps you to answer tricky questions that are usually posed during the interview process. Garnering information about the company is great to customize your answers to match the expectations of the organization. But it would be very foolhardy to offer any kind of contrary viewpoint. Such an attitude could jeopardize your chances of landing a job at the company. At the same time, the job interview is the time you and your life-changing employer are getting to know each other. It's nervous, no doubt, but be yourself and be honest about who you are and they will see if you are their next potential employee!

Chapter 3: Tell Me About Yourself

The "tell me about yourself" question is usually one of the first that are asked during a job interview. It is important for you to remember that this is not a question, which will end up in becoming best buddies with the panelists, but one that gauges your capacity as a right fit for the job.

Other forms of "tell me about yourself" could be questions such as:

- What would you like us to know about you?

Or

- What should we know about you?

If you are unsure about what aspect about you they want to discuss at this particular time in the interview process, seek clarification from them. Ask them questions like "Do you mean my work life or my approach?" This will give you more time to think, more clarity in your thought process and also set up a conversational tone to the interview process.

It is imperative to remember that the answer to this question should point to the fact that you can be a great candidate for this job. So, avoid rambling about unnecessary personal things. Stick to being as objective as you can. Avoid talking too much about your personal likes and/or dislikes, your kids and family, etc. Focus on your education, previous job experiences, and appropriate skills related to the job posting.

Prepare For This Question Beforehand

It may sound strange but you must learn about yourself before every job interview in such a way that your skills and qualifications are aligned with the requirements of the company. For this, you must do the following things:

- Go through the job description and pick out skills and experiences that meet or exceed the expectations of the company

- As you research the job and the company, make a list of your skills, your expertise, relevant experiences, unique selling points, etc. that are in line with the company's needs

- It is very important to practice your answer multiple times so that you sound natural during the interview

- Though you want to practice as much as you can, you absolutely do not want to sound scripted! Just practice as much that your answers will come out naturally like a normal conversation.

How To Answer The "Tell Me About Yourself" Question Sensibly

It makes sense to break up your answer into two sections which including how your qualifications are a good fit and the reason why you have applied for this job.

How your qualifications are a good fit – In this part, talk about how and why you chose the particular area of study. Also, make a short and succinct summary of how and why you think you are qualified for the said job. Avoid reciting data that is already there on your resume. Instead, focus on highlighting those special aspects of your experience and qualification that can give the interviewers a clearer picture of your suitability.

The reason why you have applied for this job – Here, include details of how you believe that this job will help you in advancing your career. Avoid talking about things that are not directly related to the career. Of course, it is imperative to remember at this point not to sound too unhappy about your job. It is critical to be objective and focus on how this particular job will be a great opportunity for your advancement without putting undue stress on any kind of dissatisfaction you may feel about your present job.

Make sure your reasons for applying for the job are purely professional and career-related. Do NOT use personal reasons such as:

The commute for your present job is too long for your comfort – This can be a potential put-off for many employers because they could think that if inconveniences such as daily commute are such a problem for you, then you could be intolerant of other inconveniences (which are unavoidable in the present-day working environment) as well.

You want to be home when your kids return from school – This can also be a huge deterrent again from the point of your seriousness to the work at hand.

You do not like your present boss – NEVER use this no matter how much you actually dislike him or her. These excuses reflect a highly emotional personality. Today's working environment calls for plenty of objectivity in outlook. If you are serious about your job, then personal inconveniences and likes and dislikes should not be a deterrent. Your willingness to work hard to overcome them should be clearly evident to the interviewer(s).

Examples Of Answers For "Tell Me About Yourself"

Here are some examples of good and bad answers to this all-important question.

Bad answer – I am from Connecticut and grew up wanting to be a fireman. Then, I thought I could take up health sciences. And finally, I decided, HR was going to be my realm! – Unnecessary and unrelated data are never the way to answer these introductory questions.

Good answer – I have been an HR manager for the past 10 years handling various functions and duties ranging from recruitment to benefits and rewards to training. I have worked for 3 Fortune 500 companies in the last 10 years. – Necessary and relevant data.

Final Thoughts

The ultimate goal of "tell me about yourself" is to give the interviewer(s) enough data about you so that they feel you are a good fit for the job at hand. Remember that more often than not, interviewers "want" to like a candidate sooner than later. This is because filling positions with suitable candidates is also a very daunting task for them. Assume they want to like you and then relax into giving them relevant information about yourself that singles you out from the competition.

Hiring a bad candidate reflects on the interviewers' judgment capacities, as well the people on the other side of the table are as wary and as hopeful as you are that the interview will be successful for all involved. Under these circumstances, you have to realize that what can prevent you from landing the coveted job is yourself. Maybe you're not as qualified as other job applicants. The truth is, you are competing with individuals more experience than you in the job industry. People with 5 years of total working experience or even candidates with masters or higher ed. degrees may be competing for the same job. Don't let this deter you. The job interview process is a process in which, it takes personality, work ethic, communication, and desires into consideration. Employers not only want a qualified employee to fill their position, but also they're looking for the right fit for the job. No one is exactly tailor made for the position, but if you can ace the job interview process, you can have a leg up on other candidates with more experience than you whether it'd by education or experience.

Consequently, you simply need to speak well without overdoing any aspect of the answers and use these skills and knowledge to your advantage. As you answer this seemingly innocuous "tell me about yourself" question, remember to present yourself in a way that appeals to the employer.

When you are preparing the answers, look at them from the perspective of the interviewers and see if it makes sense. Once you like what you have planned to say in answer to this question, then practice enough so that during the interview, you appear to be answering naturally and without any kind of panic.

Chapter 4: How To Avoid Common Pitfalls During Your Job Interview

There are many reasons why you may not get the job you are after and these include not being qualified enough, not being experienced enough, or even not competent enough for the job you applied for. But the most disappointing reason for not landing the job is not being prepared to avoid common mistakes that most job seekers make during the interview process.

If you have not thought about common pitfalls to avoid during the job interview, then your preparation is incomplete. So, this chapter is dedicated to giving you some common mistakes that many job seekers unwittingly make thereby losing a good chance of landing the job that they want.

Overconfidence

There is a thin line between being confident about yourself and your skills and appearing overconfident.

Employers like confidence but they abhor showing off unduly. Ensure that you avoid any kind of displays of ego or any outrageous claims. Confidence usually has a shade of humility to it. For example, if you did not know the answer to a technical question, accepting the fact that you do not know or cannot recall the precise answer at that point of time is seen as confident. But making outrageous claims and outright lying will be a huge put-off for the interviewers. So, avoid glorifying your efforts more than necessary.

Not Being Prepared

Today's interviewers are fairly ruthless against job applicants who come unprepared for the interview. The Internet is a veritable treasure house for all kinds of information and hence, hiding behind ignorance is not tolerated at all. You must do your homework regarding the company and the job you are applying for and be ready with answers for questions such as "what value can you add to the job?" or other such things of this nature. (By the way the answer to what value you can add to the job solely lies in the job description!

Being Disrespectful Or Bad Behavior

It is important to remember your manners during the entire job interview process. You cannot be disrespectful to anybody on the panel no matter what personal prejudices you may have. It is critical that you make eye contact with the person who has asked a question while answering it instead of ignoring him or her and talking only to the seemingly most important individual on the panel.

Completely avoid making frivolous jokes. Remember you are here to get a job, not to make drinking buddies. Basic courtesy and politeness are imperative aspects of your personality that must be showcased during the interview process.

Inflating Your Expertise By Lying

Yes, you are proud of what you have achieved until now, but you cannot expect yourself to know everything. It is perfectly alright to accept not knowing an answer to a question that has been asked. You could look at ways to better understand the question by reframing it or asking for more clarification before you answer it. Also by asking questions, you're showing a sense of eagerness and inquisitiveness that though you do not have the answer right now, you are interested enough in answer the questions as best you can.

However, it is unforgivable if you chose to make up answers to inflate your expertise. Do not try to guess the answers. An efficient interviewer will catch it immediately and that can spell disaster for you. Instead, simply state that you do not know! This forthrightness is appreciated by most interviewers and is definitely a better option than making up answers.

Apologizing Unduly

It is a courteous thing to apologize for a mistake. However, interviewers do not appreciate undue apologies. Saying sorry needlessly reflects an irritating lack of confidence. Moreover, apologizing often could also present you as a very weak personality and no company wants to hire a weak person. For example, instead of saying, "sorry", say "yes, but however.." or "well it seems.."

Not Asking Questions

It is a common misconception among many job seekers that asking questions could jeopardize their chances of getting the job. This is quite contrary to the true scenario. Interviewers like candidates who ask questions. Asking questions reflects your engagement in the interview process and your keenness in wanting to know more about the job.

Sensible questions that you can ask during or at the end of the interview are shown below:

•   Is the job you are applying for a newly created post?

•   Has the job position had the same job description for a long time now or is there any change? What do they expect from you?

•   Ask who you will be reporting to and who will report to you?

• You can also be forthright and ask if the interviewers feel that your qualifications fit what they are looking for.

Not Letting The Interviewers Know What And How You Intend To Contribute To The Company

While it is important to tell your interviewers how the job will help you advance in your career, you must necessarily include how you intend to contribute to the company's growth. Failing to do this reflects a one-sided and selfish personality that is not looked upon kindly by interviewers.

Complaining About Your Present Job

Do NOT EVER do this! Do not present your current employer in the wrong light. Do not talk about how difficult it is to work for your current boss. Do not complain about your present working environment.

No one wants to recruit a complaining person! Moreover, your potential employer must not get the impression that you are running from somewhere. It is far better that the interviewer thinks that you see the job as being advancement, rather than an escape route.

Answering In Monosyllables Of "Yes" Or "No," Or Rambling On Needlessly

If a question simply requires you to say yes or no, then do not ramble on! However, if the question requires a longer answer, avoid answering in monosyllables. Yet, it is critical to listen to the question and answer it precisely and succinctly without unnecessary vocabulary bravado.

Giving Practiced Answers

Yes, you need to practice your answers. But the practice should be so good that it sounds very natural to the interviewers. A "rehearsed" answer is frowned upon by most interviewers. In fact, good interviewers can catch answers that have been picked up from guidebooks. So, prepare your answers to back up your personality and experience. This will ensure that your answers do not sound practiced or rehearsed.

Dressing Sloppily

While you do not have to dress like a model or a film star, it is imperative that you present a clean, groomed look. Unkempt hair, clothes that are torn or not ironed, dirty shoes and socks that look ridiculous are an immediate put-off. Please prepare well, wear a good set of clean clothes, and appear neat and tidy at the interview.

Furthermore, wear a dress shirt and dress pants/skirt. Block out as much piercings and tattoos as much as possible. Yes, we all have our own individuality, but some employers are still old fashioned and like the clean look. Just present yourself as best as you can and because first impressions are important!

Final Thoughts

While some of the mistakes mentioned above may seem terribly basic, you would be surprised to know how many job seekers repeatedly make them unwittingly. Make sure these mistakes are deeply etched in your mind so that the avoidance of them becomes a habit rather than a conscious effort.

Chapter 5: Answers To 50 Tough Job Interview Questions

Tough questions asked during job interviews are more than likely asked to check if you can think on your feet than make you feel jittery and nervous. If you remember this trick, you will cease to be overwhelmed by the fear of answering tough questions.

Furthermore, I have asked several professionals who conduct job interviews as a requirement for their daily jobs. They include a Retail Managers, University Professors, Recruiters, Senior Directors, Consultants, and multiple CEOs. Furthermore, I have also included questions from many current working employees and asked them what has been the toughest interview question they have had and what questions did they think was the deciding factor in their current position. A holistic approach was utilized in crafting these tough interview questions to ensure quality and transparency in their nature.

This and the next chapter are dedicated to giving you some tough questions that are deliberately asked by interviewers to check out your quick-thinking capabilities. Some smart answers are also given so that you can push your mind to think along similar lines for those questions that may not be in the 50 mentioned in this book.

Once again, it is important to know that you do not memorize these answers word by word. However, familiarize your self with these answers and practice. Your preparation and understanding of certain common yet tough questions can be the difference between landing your dream job or just being another applicant.

Question 1 – What is your biggest weakness and how have you overcome it? - *I am a fairly impatient person. If things do not go perfectly when I delegate work, then it is possible for me to do the work myself. However, I ensure I do a lot of prep work so that the person to whom I delegate the work rarely falls below my expectations.*

Question 2 – Are you here to take my position? – *Yes, very much. I hope to take over your position in about 4-5 years by which time you will become the CEO and you will need a trusted person in your old job.*

Question 3 – I can see you have had plenty of jobs up until now. Are you using this job to see it fits you or are you convinced that it's the right one for you? – *At each of my earlier jobs, I have picked up essential skills that I have leveraged for the good of the company as well as the future company that I work for. I intend to use the cumulative skills to help in the growth of this company as well.*

Question 4 – How come you did not try to jump ship despite knowing that your previous company was in doldrums? – *I was working too hard at my job to notice small changes that were reflective of bigger things to come. And, moreover, with mergers happening all over in the industry, I cannot keep running away from potential layoffs. At least, I know I have given my best.*

Question 5 – There is one instance in your previous history that shows you have not got promoted despite working at the place for over 5 years. Why is that? – *Today, the company you are talking about is doing very well. However, when I was working there, layoffs were common and holding onto the job was a huge achievement. Still, the skills and knowledge that I picked up from that place are unparalleled and the* *experience was wonderful despite the glaring absence of a promotion.*

Question 6 – How come you were fired more than once from your previous jobs? – *Yes, I have been laid off twice and I was shocked both times. However, after the initial disappointment, I managed to secure better-paying and better profile jobs in both the cases.*

Question 7 – Suppose you owned a company that was manufacturing a product, which was not relevant in the market anymore, what would you do? – *I would search the globe for a new market while I encourage my engineers to tweak or change the product to suit the new demands of the existing market.*

Question 8 – You are 40-plus now. Why do you want to start at the entry level? – *It is a commonly accepted philosophy that sometimes we may have to move a step back to advance forward. And that is what I am doing. The industry I worked for until now is quite different from this and it makes a lot of sense to work my way up from the bottom to ensure that I have a total understanding of the job and can give my best to it.*

Question 9 – Why did you not join the bank where you did a short-term internship? Did your performance during the internship not meet their expectations? – *Yes, I did complete an internship at the bank mentioned and it was a highly successful one. I have recommendation letters that prove how well the people appreciated my performance. However, when I completed my course, the bank was laying off many employees and hiring was frozen. Today, I believe that this seemingly unlucky break was actually a lucky one since I was compelled to look elsewhere and that's what brought me to this job interview.*

Question 10 – While we love diversity in our company, for this particular position, which involves interacting with Southeast Asian countries, however, we are keen on recruiting Asian males. – How would you as a white female, deal with this type of diversity if you were to get hired? – *I have learned a great deal with the Asian culture and many of my friends are that of Asian descent. I love working with many diverse people and I believe my skills and background would translate well with working with this particular group of people, as well as, being successful in this particular position.*

Question 11 – Why did you have to take such a long break from work? Why do you want to get back to work now? – *I quit my job earlier for the sake of my newborn baby. My spouse was on a 24/7 job and one of us had to sacrifice time for our child and I chose to. Now, that my child is old enough to manage independently, I am happy to get back to work as I really miss the work. (It is important to tell the truth and not an excuse. Just be frank, while also being appropriate while answering the question. For example, saying you had personal or a family tragedy for instance, is completely fine to say. Remember to not ramble about personal stories. Keep it succinct and professional.*

OR

I had family and health emergencies I needed to tend to before I wanted to start work again. By taking care of those I love first, I can then focus on my career because my family has provided so much for me.

Question 12 – We are an ethnic company and all our customers are more comfortable with ethnic people rather than people like you. Hence, I am hesitating to hire you. – *As a writer, the one qualification that is as important as my writing skills is to have empathy. If you were to look beyond my skin color, you would see my high level of experience and qualifications* *and would appreciate that your company and your customers would gain from their interaction with me.*

Question 13 – Suppose you want to hire a woman for a job in your team and your boss wants a man in that position. What would you do? – *I would hire both on a two-week trial basis as freelancers and make the choice after experimenting with both.*

Question 14 – How would you handle a situation in which the person you are working with takes all credit? – *I would first publicly credit her own ideas as this will kind of make her obliged to return the favor. Otherwise, we could arrange to present each of our ideas separately to the boss. I could openly discuss my feelings of resentment and arrive at an amicable solution.*

Question 15 – How many hours can you put in each week? – *I usually work long hours. During the additional time I work, I try and see if there are some improvements I can make for my clients. When customers see my work, they are left with no doubt that it is my company that has done their work.*

Question 16 – Do you think it is good for a company to have only A players on its payroll? – *No, I believe it is better to have a balanced set of A and B players on the payroll. This is because it is highly likely that too many A players can create undue and harmful friction leading to more losses than gains for the company. Moreover, while A players run the customer interface, the B players can focus on hammering out the ops details which are critical to the success of any company.*

Question 17 – Are you a "managing up" person or a "managing down" person? – *I personally believe that if I do not know how to do the former, I can never be successful with the latter. I am flexible can manage both ways.*

Question 18 – Would you get permission from your boss to try out something new or would you like to be free from such red-tape measures? – *To me, it's always important to ask my supervisor if it's okay to venture out new assignments or tasks that would help the company perform better. After some time have past, maybe 6 months, and building good rapport with my supervisor, I would only try out something new if I were fully confident if it would impact the company in a positive direction.*

Question 19 – Give us an example of how you managed a tricky situation at one of your previous jobs – *When my first boss hired me, he had already planned to retire within a few days after he hired me. He simply passed on all his assignments to me. I completed the assignments and left them on his desk a week prior his resignation. I also forwarded the same completed assignments to the new boss to ensure a smooth transition to my new supervisor. This kept both the boss and the other people content.*

Question 20 – What do you think is more important for success in the workplace; skill or luck? – *I think it is normal for people to say that skill is more important than luck for success. However, I have always believed that both aspects play an important role in the success of an individual. You need luck for good opportunities to come along and you need the skill to grab and hold onto some of those opportunities. Furthermore, I believe luck arises when skill, practice, and perseverance have occurred.*

Question 21 – At what age do you think you will reach a peak in your performance? – *As I come from a family of mentally, physically and emotionally healthy people, I have never thought of "peaking" at any point. However, I do understand that advancing*

age can give you the maturity to step down at a time
when someone is ready to take over from you.

Question 22 – When do you think it is right to break
a confidence? – *I will not hesitate to break the*
confidence of a friend or colleague if he or she has
confided in me that he/she has done something
illegal.

Question 23 – Do you believe you are a leader? –
Yes, undoubtedly. I am a great listener but can talk
sense into people as well. I love following big ideas
but also know when to be practical and sensible.

Question 24 – What do you see as a disadvantage in
the position you have applied for? – *I believe that*
collaborating with people from different time zones
and geographical zones is going to be a challenge.
However, modern-day collaborative tools such as
video conferencing, faxes, emails, etc. will easily help
me overcome these challenges.

Question 25 – Can you give an example of an
unpopular decision you took? – *At one workplace, I*

had a boss who managed four different offices and was really short on time. He wanted me to play the role of a quasi-boss during his absence. I did not agree to this as I already knew the fate of several quasi-bosses that he had appointed unofficially with neither a new formal contract nor an official announcement.

Despite knowing that this would anger him, I flatly refused, saying that I would take on the role only if he made an official announcement and made suitable changes in my contract. It did make my life more difficult than before at that office, but I am glad that I chose to be upfront and honest with my boss rather than agree to present an ingratiating attitude.

Chapter 6: Answers To 50 Tough Job Interview Questions (Continued)

Question 26 – What would be your definition of a dream job? – *This (current job you applied for) is what I hope and believe will be my dream job. I intend to use all my skills and knowledge gained until now for the growth and development of this company.*

Question 27 – How much do you participate in internal politics? – *I would be naïve if I told you that I am not aware of internal politics in any organization. However, I am also sensible enough to recognize the traits of a hardcore internal politician in an organization and steer clear of the person as much as possible. If the person involved is my own boss or is on my team, then I would make an attempt to be honest and tell him I do not like to nor have the requisite skills to be part of any internal office politics.*

Question 28 – What personality trait would you describe yourself? – *I believe I am hardworking and efficient individual. I'm mostly a 'get the job' done type of person but I am easy going as well.*

Question 29 – Do you have any pet peeves? – *If you ask my college roommate, he would probably say the mess in his part of the room or the volume of the music he plays. Other than this, I do not carry any pet peeves. I am rationally mature enough to take a moment and step back during those worrying times and find solutions by looking at "peeves" objectively.*

Question 30 – If you had the chance to relive the last 10 years of your life, what would you do differently? – *I do not want to change anything in my life as even the toughest times taught me huge lessons and without those lessons, I would not be where I am today; happy and satisfied. Having said that, 10 years ago, I realized that I was an inherently lazy person. I would have loved to correct that aspect of my personality earlier but took the necessary action to become much more proactive.*

Question 31 – In what ways do you handle stress? – *I love music and am learning to play the piano. My biggest stress buster has been listening to music.*

When I am at home and can play the piano, I do use my playing to relieve stress. I also enjoy reading thrillers and solving murder mysteries helps me relieve stress. In an office environment, I simply go for a 10-minute walk in the outdoors to shake off stress.

Question 32 – What motivates you? – *A hardworking team motivates me greatly. I am motivated by the applause I get when I do a presentation well. I am motivated by results and enthusiastic to do more. Learning new things works always motivate me to get things done right.*

Question 33 – Have your mistakes taught you any lesson? – *Oh yes, my mistakes were my most successful teachers. The lessons from my mistakes have made me very sensitive to issues that may sneak up on me. I have learned to be keenly aware of these stealthy issues and have learned to counter them well. My mistakes have taught me more humility, more restraint and more tolerance towards others' mistakes.*

Question 34 – What do you get most criticized about? – *I had a boss in an earlier organization that believed that I was too critical of other people's work.*

This was a revelation, as until then I believed I was helping someone get better at what he or she was doing. I have since learned more patience.

That is when I realized that correcting other people's work too often might not be a great idea. So, I changed tactics. I first said the good things and then took time to point out how some other things could have been done better. Since then, I have not had the same issues.

Question 35 – What is your greatest disappointment to this present date? – (Note to reader: It is good not to use office matters for this question.) Use more personal disappointments such as: *My biggest disappointment was that I was not able to follow my passion to become a professional singer or I still feel sad that I lost my dad before he could see me graduate.*

Question 36 – What is the worst thing you have done and managed to get away with? – (Note to reader: Keep the answer informal and light. It is better to make a joke of it like saying how you pulled an amazing prank on your classmate and how nobody knows it was you who did it.) You can use a good deed you did as well, though this might come out as more condescending than you would like. So, it is prudent to stick to something mischievous that happened in college or when you were younger.

When I was in elementary school in 2nd grade, I use to struggle during math class and when the report card came, we had to have our parents sign it and return to the teachers. Needless to say, since I was disappointed at myself, I forged my parent's signature on the report card. Being naïve, I was caught by my teachers and parents and I was grounded for 2 weeks! I realized what I was doing was wrong, but that experience helped me fully understand the gravity of responsibility.

Question 37 – How did you solve problems in your previous jobs? – (Note to reader: For this, be prepared with a couple of answers along with detailed explanations. It would be nice to elaborate a little though it is equally important to ask permission if the time taken to answer this question is going to be longer than normal.)

I would arrive early in the morning just to get settled and then the first thing I would do is to look at my calendar and daily tasks I would need to accomplish for my day. Usually, if there were any problems I would encounter, I would first try to solve the issue on my own before asking my coworkers and supervisors. Depending on the problem and once I resolved the issue, I would take notes on and write down steps for future related problems to ensure efficiency when the same issue arises again.

Question 38 – What do you dislike about your current job? – (Note to reader: Again avoid complaining about anything or anybody. Simply convert your negative feelings into positive ones and then answer the question. You could say that the team you work with and your supervisor are great and you are enjoying working there.)

The only thing I believe I do not like in the current job is that there is nothing left to challenge me. I like new challenges that will enable met to use my mind and also, keep things fresh around the office space. Tasks that I have successfully completed can get mundane so I like finding new challenges that will make me become a better employee.

Question 39 – Who was your worst boss and who was your best? – *I do not believe any one of my bosses was bad in any specific way. Yes, some were more challenging to work for than others. Honestly, I do not have any favorites. But I have learned from each one of them how to manage a team of people from varied backgrounds and varied skill sets.*

Question 40 – Do you think you are the best qualified for this job and why? – *My ability to work unsupervised and my educational qualifications make me an ideal candidate for the job at hand. Along with my work ethic and passion to be part of a great company like this one, I do believe I am the perfect fit for this position.*

Question 41 – How would you like to describe your career goals? – (Note to reader: It might be a good idea to start with short-term goals and then move on to the long-term goals. Explain how you plan to achieve these goals and do not hesitate to include any courses that you would like to take to achieve these professional goals.)

My career goals include working for a mid sized engineering company like yours, and gaining valuable work and business experience to work up the company ranks such as managerial and director positions. Furthermore, I would like to enhance my computer technical skills like many of the senior directors here by learning how to use Oracle. I would take an online course and gain the proper certification to achieve this.

Question 42 – What is your work style? – (Note to reader: For this, you can use one or more of the following styles to explain how you work):

Speed and accuracy – If you are known for speed and accuracy and can work efficiently and without errors, mention this now. Say something like: *"When doing tedious tasks, I tend to start out at slower pace to make sure I understand the process completely. After it becomes second nature, my work style is typically quick, but also accurate."*

How you structure your day – Explain how you plan and schedule your day. *You can talk about which jobs you like to do in the mornings and which of them you like to do later in the day. Here, you can also mention how many hours you work in a typical day.*

Whether you are a better collaborator or prefer working alone – *Answer this question after due thought. Almost all jobs have some amount of collaboration with others and hence if you do prefer working alone, do not emphasize it too much. Instead, say that you are flexible and can work in both environments.*

Question 43 - Do you take your work home? – *You need not give an outright "yes" or "no" answer.* It would more prudent to mention your flexibility in this aspect and say that you are willing to take work home if it makes sense to do so. *However, also mention that, in a typical workday, you are most likely at the office/building/cubicle and that you are always willing to come to the office if needed.* This type of question will solely depend if your employer allows you to work from home.

Question 44 – What is your measure of success? – *I measure success depending on the scenario. At work, success would mean promotions, added responsibilities and more income. On the personal front, success could mean spending quality time with family and friends. Success could also mean being remembered for giving your best shot at everything you do.*

Question 45 – How long do you plan to work for our firm? – *You need not give a straightforward answer to this although you must not give a short-term and dishonest answer. Instead, you can focus on what appeals to you about the job and the reason why you applied for this specific job. You could mention the aspects of the job that could motivate you into staying longer.*

Question 46 – What is your next step? – *I believe in taking small and sure steps. So, once I have established my position and reputation in this company, then I would like to look further. At the moment, working on giving my best to this job is going to be my only focus.*

Question 47 - How are you going to contribute to this company? – *To answer this question, you must include it in the researching that you do on the job and the company. With data collected during the research, you will be able to find information that will help you form a good answer for this question. While qualifications and skills are established things, you must be a little more specific in answering this question and explain exactly how you think your work will help in the growth and development of this company.*

Question 48 – Can you tell us what you know about our company? – *The answer to this question also needs some amount of research. Do not go unprepared to answer this question. Rehearse and practice the answer well so that your interviewers are impressed with your knowledge. If there's one answer you must rehearse, it's this one! Furthermore, questions like these are often asked in a* *different way so if there's one question that you must prepare for, this one takes the cake!*

Example: Interviewing for an Accounting position for Grant Thornton.

I really think "Grant Thornton" is providing top notch accounting services such as audits and tax services for midsized and large businesses located in the local Chicago area. By ensuring accuracy, professionalism, and expertise in upholding business regulations, Grant Thornton has become the very best in terms of an accounting institution in the United States. The company is always rated as one of the best accounting firms across the nation and in 2017.

A company like this is something I want to be part of and I believe I will fit right in with my educational background and work experience. I also think I can have a profound impact in not only sustaining the reputation of this company, but also enhancing efficiency in whole accounting process. My goal is to improve the quality of accounting services that Grant Thornton provides to its customers.

Question 49 – What do you believe is your biggest strength? – *I have a strong work ethic and when a job is entrusted to me, I will not simply try to finish it well before the deadline, but also in the best possible way. In fact, this has earned me bonuses for several years as I have completed 3-4 projects every year at least a week before the deadline.*

Question 50 – What if you do not get this job? – *Well, I am not one to be discouraged easily. I will request feedback and learn from my mistakes and move on in life. Also, I will continue to keep a lookout for any openings in this company because, now it is exceedingly clear to me that the values of this company are in alignment with my own.*

Final Thoughts

You must remember that these questions are only indicators. They could be asked in different formats or be variations on similar themes. So, while you practice answers to these questions, please be aware that you may need to think on your feet and come up with some witty or smart answers during the job interview process.

Chapter 7: Preparing For The Job Interview

While all the things that you do before an interview are part of the preparation, it is nice to have a ready-to-use checklist. So, I thought it made sense to have one chapter dedicated to this checklist.

Be Prepared

This includes researching the job and the company by finding out as much information as you can from friends, present employees and the ever-friendly Internet. Be ready with all the answers to the questions that are likely to be asked about the job and the company

Understand And Know Your Skills, Experience And Qualifications In Relation To The Job You Are Applying For

It is very likely that you know all about your technical and soft skills, the experience you have gained, and how your qualifications helped you perform well in your professional life. Yet, it is imperative that you align these skills, experience, and qualifications in such a way that you can answer questions that are related to the job you have applied for.

For example, you must prepare an answer based on your skills and expertise to the question of how you are going to contribute to the organization. You must be able to convince the interviewers that you can use your expertise to do the job better than the way it was done before.

Make A List Of Questions That You Will Ask The Interviewers

This book gives you a list of sensible questions you can ask the interviewers. Crystallize this strategy with the good list ready at hand.

Be ready with relevant material including documents that you may need for the interview

Keeping these things ready will reduce any kind of last-minute pressure. Make a folder where you will keep all the necessary documents such as certificates, recommendation letters, etc. Keep the original as well as a couple of copies of each so that you can hand a full set of documents across the table if asked.

Eat Well, Sleep Well And Wake Up Early On The Day Of The Interview

Hunger and fatigue due to lack of sleep and stress are a deadly combination for panic. Be aware that such a situation can arise and counter it in by making sure you eat well, sleep early so that you get at least 6-7 hours of sleep the day before the interview, and set the alarm early. Do not get up late and increase the panic situation.

Try and go for a morning walk or jog to relax yourself. Have a healthy breakfast and get to the interview venue at least 15 minutes before time. Do not rush at the last minute. In the 15 minutes, try and gauge the environment. After this, simply relax with some deep breathing exercises.

Dress Well

Ensure you get your clothes ready the day before, all neatly ironed and laid out for the morning. This way, your clothes will not be crumpled and your overall profile will be very professional thereby creating a good first impression on the interviewers.

Arrive On Time (AKA 15 minutes early!)

This should be a no brainer. Arriving on time is a given courtesy that all potential employees should have. Make a good impression and arrive early! Arriving on time means arriving 15 minutes before hand. Fifteen minutes early is perfect because it will allow you to search for the exact location or office if you are unfamiliar with the building. Furthermore, the day before, program your phone, GPS, reminder, and calendar event the exact address of your job interview. Remember, first impressions are important and if you're not there on time for your job interview, chances are you're not on time to get a job offer!

And Finally, Do Not Panic

The interviewers are human beings like you and they want to get a good candidate as much as you want to get a good job. And remember, the worst thing that can happen is that you will not get this job. Well, won't there be other opportunities if this fails? Do not panic and fret and allow a good opportunity to slip by due to the panic-driven clouding of your thinking process. Stay calm, and believe it or not, try to have fun.

It shouldn't be a torturous experience, rather, treat it as just a formal sit down talk about yourself, the employer, and how you will be a great candidate for the job. It's not the end of the world if you do not get a job. If you think about it, ask all the people you know. I bet 99% of the people you know have either been rejected for a job they applied for or did not hear back from a certain prospective position. It's not so much as a failure if you do not get the job you want, but rather it's a growing experience that you should take note of and improve upon your next job interview. However, the tips provided in this book will hopefully give you an edge to other job seekers that will make you stand out and land the job that suits you the best. Stay persistent and the right opportunity will knock at the right time.

Chapter 8: How To Sell Yourself

Selling yourself is a key ingredient in landing the coveted job. So, this chapter deals with some tips that will help you sell yourself at the job interview.

Know Your Brand

Think of a company brand like Coca-Cola, KFC, etc. What makes their products sell so well is the knowledge of their brand. Likewise, understand your brand and what values, mission, and principles make you the person you are. When you are clear about your brand and the passion for the job at hand will also emerge and this passion will be reflected in the interview process leaving no doubt in the minds of the interviewers of who you are.

Learn To Tell A Story

Your job experiences, your educational qualifications, your life at college and all other relevant information about you should be woven like a beautiful story that the interviewers will enjoy hearing. Be enthusiastic when you are answering questions and let your story sound exciting and interesting. Let your excitement come across in an authentic and natural manner.

Know The Company And The Interview Panel

Know all about the company, the interview panel and the industry in general so that you can easily tell your story moving from one aspect to another in a seamless manner. Be aware of the recent events and happenings and create a good campaign for yourself.

Present Visuals And Not Just Words

Create an image in the minds of the interviewers about your experiences instead of merely talking words. Use examples as much as possible so that your explanation is illustrative. Speak of your experiences and not merely about dull certifications and qualifications. It will be easy for the interviewers to link your skills to your expertise.

Apply For Jobs Where There Is A Match Between The Job, The Company, And Your Own Brand

Match your brand and only apply once you know the job is a perfect fit. If there is going to be a mismatch between your values, mission and purpose with that of the company you are planning to work in, a disastrous end is bound to happen sooner than later. If you cannot clearly see the match, then continue looking for jobs. As tedious as the job search maybe, know that the perfect job is out there for you waiting to be discovered. It's just a matter of putting in the work in researching the right job for your skills and experience.

Chapter 9: Salary Negotiation

Negotiating your salary is part and parcel of a job interview process. Of course, this aspect may be the last thing on the list before you are finally selected for the job.

Things You Need To Know About Salaries

Every position in most medium-large companies has a pay range and not necessarily a fixed pay. The pay difference at a junior level will be about 20% between the highest and the lowest in that range.

While most organizations target the lower half of the range while recruiting new people, they are also willing to go up to the upper half depending on the skills and expertise of the candidate.

You must compare the market pricing of the position you are applying for and your offer. It may not be correct to compare the new offer with your old salary.

Do not expect the recruiting consultant to negotiate your pay for you. You will have to do it yourself if you are keen. Don't undersell yourself.

And finally, remember that once you are employed, then pay reviews may not happen as promised, owing to freezes and conservative budgets. Hence, it is better to negotiate *before* you are employed.

Tips On How To Negotiate Your Salary

Know what the salary is – Be aware of how much you expect your salary to be. Invariably, you will be asked about your expectations in an initial screening so that the employer understands that it is within the range they are looking at. At this stage, the company might choose not to shortlist you based on this information.

Be aware of the market range – There are many consultant agencies who have statistics about salaries for various positions on the market. In the next section, various resources/websites for salary negotiations and salary range will be discussed. It is better to avoid making assumptions based on bragging by employees on social media websites.

Know WHEN To Negotiate During The Interview Process – It would be foolhardy if you chose to negotiate your salary early during the recruitment phase. Hold on until you are sure you are the preferred candidate and then use this power to negotiate a better salary. And even then, do not talk about pay in an immature manner. Speak to them and tell them that you are aware of what the market range is and ask whether the company will be able to match the market range.

Remember to compare things that are reasonable – It would be naïve to compare oranges with apples. Compare what is being offered to you vs the market range. This range need not necessarily be comparable to your pay package in your earlier firm or any other position in the company. Find out what other benefits are included, how much is a fixed component and how much is based on performance. If a component is based on performance, you must be clearly aware of whether it is your individual performance or your team performance or the performance of the company in general that dictates how much you get.

Location, Location, Location – The salary of certain positions highly depends on location. For example, if you're looking into a Physical Therapist position in Mansfield, Ohio, the median salary is about $73,000. While the same position in Los Angeles, California is $89,681. Along with your experience, location plays a big role so knowing these types of geographical statistics will play a role in your salary negotiation.

Resources for Salary Negotiation

Again, websites such as Glassdoor and Indeed.com are simply one of the best when it comes to researching job positions and especially about their salary range. Use this as a great guide when you're doing your salary negotiations. Other resources I would recommend are local university sites within your region. For example, using the Physical Therapist position in Los Angles, take a look UCLA or other universities within the area and go to their Physical Therapy website department. About 90% of colleges and universities will have a page that states salary ranges for professionals for that specific job position. Again, keep in mind that this is a range. In the Physical Therapy position in Los Angeles, though the median is $89,000, if you're just starting to work, expect about $5,000 less of what the median makes. So a brand new graduate with a Doctor's of Physical Therapy in Los Angeles can expect to make around $78,000-$84,000. Likewise, if you're moving to Los Angeles from out of state and you have 5+ years of experience, expect to make $5,000 more than the median so about $90,000-$95,000. (great salary by the way!)

Finally, remember that with regards to salary negotiations, you will not get more if you do not ask. You only have to ask in a REASONABLE fashion and as politely as you can. And if you think the compensation is not good enough and you are willing to wait for another opportunity to come up, do not hesitate to say so politely. It will be greatly appreciated. There's never harm in asking, but doing so graciously, employers will respect it and will also bring up other related topics to negotiations, such as bonuses, vacations, medical, stocks, and other forms of compensation.

Conclusion

The winning is never in the performance, it is in the practice – an English proverb says. Thus, if you practice hard, work hard and prepare well for an upcoming job interview, the chances of failing are very low. Moreover, even if you are faced with a couple of failures you can rest assured that the learning you picked up while preparing for the job interview will always remain with you.

The more you prepare, the more the chances of success. The most important thing that I would like to reiterate in the concluding chapter is never to panic. Fear is a highly debilitating emotion that prevents clear thinking. In a panic mode, even the simplest of questions will appear difficult and answers will evade you. So, do not panic.

So, let me end by summarizing the preparatory stage:

• Write a good and professional resume and a compelling cover letter

- Research the job and the company well so that the information will help you during the interview process

- Practice the art of answering smartly and sensibly without being overtly friendly with the interviewers

- Know what the market salary structure is like for the position you are applying and base your negotiations around it

- Make sure you get a good night's sleep, eat a healthy breakfast and present a professional profile to the interviewers.

Being successful in a job interview is not rocket science. It is only a matter of being aware of what to expect, practice for it, and also be prepared for the unexpected. So, hold your head high and walk into the interview confidently.

Citations

http://career-advice.careerone.com.au/job-interview-tips/interview-preparation/ten-tips-preparing-for-job-interview/article.aspx

http://www.right.com/wps/wcm/connect/right-us-en/home/thoughtwire/categories/career-work/10-salary-negotiation-tips-to-use-on-the-way-in

http://www.telegraph.co.uk/finance/jobs/11237738/The-13-most-common-job-interview-mistakes.html

www.glassdoor.com

www.indeed.com

BCPL
Baltimore County
Public Library

Made in the USA
Columbia, SC
04 August 2017